A History of Punk

From It's Origins to the Present

By Lora Greene

BOOKCAPS

BookCaps™ Study Guides

www.bookcaps.com

© 2012. All Rights Reserved.

Table of Contents

ABOUT HISTORYCAPS 4

INTRODUCTION..5

CHAPTER 1: THE BIRTH OF PUNK 6

GARAGE ROCK AND THE BRITISH INVASION 7
Garage Rock/ British Invasion Essential Tracks: *12*
BOWIE, IGGY AND LOU REED - GLAM ROCK AND THE GUTTER 13
Glam/Proto-Punk Essential Tracks: *17*

CHAPTER 2: BUILDING AN EMPIRE OF DESTRUCTION 18

LET'S BUILD A HOME: CBGB AND THE ROXY 19
CBGB and The Roxy Essential Tracks:............................*24*
THE SEX PISTOLS: THE FILTH, THE FURY AND THE FASHION 25
Sex Pistols and Friends Essential Tracks: *30*
LIKE WILDFIRE: PUNK ROCK SPREADS ACROSS THE WORLD 31
International Punk Rock Essential Tracks: *37*
THE ONLY BAND THAT MATTERS: THE CLASH BREAK THE MOLD..38
The Clash Essential Tracks:...*43*

CHAPTER 3: TURNING SOUND INTO A DOLLAR SIGN 44

SELLING OUT AND CASHING IN: THE GO GO'S, BILLY IDOL AND THE POLICE 45
Punk Rock Sellouts Essential Tracks................................*50*

CHAPTER 4: NEW WAVE...51

AND I RAN: NEW WAVE AND POST-PUNK............................52
New Wave/ Post-Punk Essential Tracks: *57*
BIG A, LITTLE A: ANARCHO-PUNK 58
Anarcho-Punk Essential Tracks:......................................*63*
OUT OF STEP WITH THE WORLD: HARDCORE AND OI! 64
Hardcore, Oi! and Street Punk Essential Tracks:............*68*

CHAPTER 5: THE REBIRTH OF PUNK 69

SELF ESTEEM: THE PUNK ROCK REVIVAL 70
Punk Revival Essential Tracks: 75
A MESSAGE TO YOU, RUDY: 2 TONE AND SKA-PUNK 76
2 Tone and Ska-Punk Essential Tracks: 79

CHAPTER 6: PUNK...PRESENT AND FUTURE 80

I WAS A TEENAGE ANARCHIST: EMO, SCREAMO AND PUNK
ROCK TODAY 81
Emo, Screamo and Punk Rock Today Essential Tracks:..86

About HistoryCaps

HistoryCaps is an imprint of BookCaps™ Study Guides. With each book, a brief period of history is recapped. We publish a wide array of topics (from baseball and music to science and philosophy), so check our growing catalogue regularly (**www.bookcaps.com**) to see our newest books.

Introduction

In the waning days of the 20th century, disaffected kids with no prospects accidentally started a revolution. What began as a new way to pass the time would go on to influence thousands, maybe even millions of people across the world, people who had been left behind by a world obsessed with a pretty narrow notion of success. Some of these kids became household names, some of them became nothing remarkable, but all of them were forever changed by this strange new music called punk rock.

Where did punk rock come from? Where is it going? There are a hundred different answers to these questions, none of them right or wrong. But maybe by exploring some of the signposts along the way, this book will shed a little light on what punk rock meant to the people whose lives were changed by it. Whether first discovered in 1977, 1989, or 2012 (and beyond), punk rock meant a lot of different things to a lot of different people. Lester Bangs, the legendary music writer and early supporter of punk rock, summed it up more succinctly than most:

"At its best, punk represents a fundamental and age-old Utopian dream: that if you give people the license to be as outrageous as they want in absolutely any fashion they can dream up, they'll be creative about it, and do something good besides."

Chapter 1: The Birth of Punk

Garage Rock and The British Invasion

While the true origin of punk rock has been a topic of heated debate in certain circles, practically since the term was coined, one listen to any of the thousands of one-off garage rock singles that sprung out of the post-war American suburbs makes it pretty clear.

For the first time in history, huge numbers of young families packed up and moved away from crime-ridden cities all across the USA in search of a new American Dream. Predictably, their children got bored pretty quickly, and with the disposable income afforded this newly-minted middle class, a lot of these kids begged for electric guitars and drum sets. A fuse was lit.

These kids retreated to their garages and formed raw, visceral bands with names like The Seeds, The Electric Prunes and The Knickerbockers. Most of these teenagers had little idea how to play their newly gifted instruments, but that certainly didn't stop them. They performed at school dances and county fairs, and a lot of them recorded a song or two in a real live recording studio before disbanding, growing up and getting real jobs. These bands mostly had the records pressed themselves in small batches and sold them for a dollar or two at their shows, presaging the DIY movement by decades. Only a few groups garnered any commercial success: The Kingsmen hit the charts in 1963 with the ubiquitous *Louie, Louie*. The Trashmen had a sizeable seller with *Surfin' Bird*.

The main thing that separated these groups from the popular acts of the day was geography. While big cities like New York, Los Angeles and Detroit were home to some of the best-selling rock n roll groups, most of the garage rock bands originated in second-tier cities. The Knickerbockers hailed from Bergenfield, New Jersey. The Shadows of Knight were from Arlington Heights, Illinois. The members of Nazz were the pride and joy of Philadelphia, Pennsylvania.

Despite its limited commercial appeal, record company bigwigs still tried to co-opt and repackage the authentic garage rock sound into something a little more palatable for mainstream audiences. The Strangeloves were a notable case. A trio of professional New York City songwriters, the group created an impressive backstory, pretending their band was comprised of a group of rural Australian brothers who had gotten rich inventing a new hybrid sheep. With money and time to spare, they decided to form a band, resulting in the top 10 hit *I Want Candy*. Ironically, the band's music failed to chart in their "native" Australia. One member, Richard Gottehrer, went on to cofound Sire Records, future home of trailblazing punk bands The Ramones, Blondie and Talking Heads.

Nobody quite knows how many of these early garage rock bands are utterly lost to history. One thing that's clear: were it not for the efforts of one man, Lenny Kaye, the number would be a lot higher. Kaye, alongside Elektra Records founder Jac Holzman, worked together to create the first (and most popular) collection of these forgotten gems. Released in 1972, the two-record set called *Nuggets* would have a profound influence on punk rock, reminding all who heard it that the best music doesn't necessarily come from the greatest musicians. All anyone truly needed was a few chords and a whole lot of energy. Lenny Kaye's name comes up again as a founding member of The Patti Smith Group, one of the more influential proto-punk bands to come out of mid 70's New York.

The sound and the fury of 60's garage rock can still be heard today on records by critically-acclaimed bands like The White Stripes, The Strokes and The Black Keys. These bands led an early 2000s garage rock revival, selling millions of records (and winning a few Grammy Awards in the process.)

You've seen the tape: screaming, fainting teenage girls drowning out the sound of The Beatles on Ed Sullivan. Beatlemania, to the untrained eye, looks pretty much the same as Bieber Fever, but something *different* was brewing. By 1965, a full-fledged sonic invasion was underway. Just like in America, British kids with nothing to do and little in the way of future prospects started banging away in their garages, making a racket that would soon reverberate around the world.

While The Beatles seemed to be nothing more than a marketing department's wet dream, the next crop of British bands literally drew the blueprint for punk rock. Working from a template of early American blues filtered through a haze of amphetamines, The Who, The Zombies and The Small Faces were pioneers in snarling, dangerous music. They didn't want to hold your hand; they just hoped they'd die before they got old. When punk rock first took off in England, The Who were one of the only groups of the era that bands like The Sex Pistols and The Clash didn't openly despise. In Fact, The Pistols even recorded pretty fantastic versions of The Who's *Substitute* and The Small Faces' *What'cha Gonna Do About it*.

It's impossible to overstate the importance of British bands in America in the mid-60s. US affinity for all things Great Britain reached a fever pitch on May 9th, 1965, when British rock groups so dominated the US singles chart that nine of the top ten songs were from the UK. That extraordinary feat hadn't ever happened before, and it's pretty unlikely that it will ever happen again.

The Kinks, quite possibly the best of all the British Invasion bands of the mid-60's, never made much headway in the US. While an early single, *You Really Got Me*, is a staple on classic rock radio, the group were never able to capitalize on its initial success. They were banned from touring in the United States from 1964 to 1968. While no reason was ever given, it's widely assumed that their frenetic, often violent stage show was deemed a threat to American audiences. Now that's punk rock.

Garage Rock/ British Invasion Essential Tracks:

1. Don't Come Around - Trolls
2. I Got My Mojo Workin' - The Shadows of Knight
3. Louie, Louie - The Kingsmen
4. Psycho - The Sonics
5. Laugh, Laugh - The Beau Brummels
6. She's Not There - The Zombies
7. Substitute - The Who
8. We Gotta Get Out of This Place - The Animals
9. Gloria - Them (W/ Van Morrison)
10. What'cha Gonna Do About It - The Small Faces

Bowie, Iggy and Lou Reed - Glam Rock and the Gutter

Nobody was more pertinent to the development of punk than the "unholy triumvirate" of David Bowie, Iggy Pop and Lou Reed. While all three are wildly influential on their own, the three men are forever linked as the brightest signposts on the road to punk rock.

Bowie was a commercially unsuccessful pop crooner who reinvented himself as a space-traveling weirdo. Though only mildly successful in America, David Bowie was a bona fide rock god in his native Great Britain. Beginning with the 1968 release of *Space Oddity*, Bowie virtually invented the glam rock scene.

Characterized by restrained, cathartic rock n roll with a theatrical bent, glam rock had become a national obsession in the UK by the early 70s, led by Bowie and other bands like T. Rex, Roxy Music and Slade. Each subsequent album (and costume change) upped the outlandishness ante until unbridled weirdness was the norm. Imagine roving gangs of British teenagers dressed for Halloween every single waking moment. Platform heels, heavy makeup (for girls *and* boys), feathers, leotards; it was all permitted. Early punk bands like Siouxsie and The Banshees and The Damned wouldn't have existed without glam rock's theatrical influence.

The fun spread to America in a limited way but never quite caught on. Alice Cooper took glam rock's theatricality and melded it with a low-rent horror movie aesthetic. The New York Dolls were a glam rock band, but they were far too ugly and masculine to fully pull it off. Malcolm Mclaren, manager of The New York Dolls, would go on to be instrumental in the story of punk rock: he put together the lineup that would become The Sex Pistols, the first true punk band (depending on who you ask).

Iggy Pop, on the other hand, was decidedly un-glam. Leader of The Stooges, an influential proto-punk band from Detroit, he was a violent, drug-addled lunatic who would often cut himself during live performances. Alongside another Detroit band, The MC5, The Stooges crafted a "wall of feedback" sound as violent and scary as Iggy's onstage persona. Songs like *I Wanna Be Your Dog* and *T.V. Eye* were among the heaviest records to have ever been released.

Though their records sold poorly, especially in America, they were so well-regarded among the tastemakers of the time that David Bowie himself produced their third (and final) album, *Raw Power*. Archetypal leather-clad, unpredictable punk rockers like Sid Vicious and Darby Crash were cut whole from the Iggy Pop cloth. Incidentally, Pop is also credited with the invention of stage diving.

Lou Reed was the driving force behind The Velvet Underground, an Andy Warhol-affiliated avant garde rock band. There is an oft-cited quote about the band that bears repeating: while fewer than 10,000 people bought their first record, every single one of them went on to form a band. It's obviously apocryphal, but the point is totally valid. Songs like *Venus in Furs* and *Heroin* were shocking in both their subject matter and their execution. That penchant for writing about traditionally taboo subjects would have a profound influence on the punk rock movement.

When the band broke up, Reed reinvented himself as a genderbending gutter poet and earned the nickname "The Godfather of Punk", mostly by going out his way to subvert his fans' expectations on albums like 1973's thoroughly depressing *Berlin and* 1975's *Metal Machine Music*, an experiment in feedback-generated sounds that was entirely devoid of structure and lyrics. Widely derided at the time, *Metal Machine Music* is now seen as a precursor to post-punk and industrial music, although everyone is still pretty sure that Lou Reed was just making fun of his audience and trying to piss off his record label. Reed's most popular song, the excellent *Walk on the Wild Side*, released in 1972, was a worldwide radio hit, despite repeated references to drugs, oral sex and male prostitution.

Lou Reed remains one of the most polarizing artists of the last 50 years. Though he undoubtedly influenced countless bands, from the sneering, snotty by-the-numbers punk of Eater and The Adverts to the dark, twisted poetry of Joy Division, he still has the power to shock and offend. In 2011, he released the universally hated album *Lulu*, a collaboration with noted metal band Metallica. Most reviewers gave the album zero stars, while Reed held a press conference, informing everyone that Metallica had inspired him to

new artistic heights. "They pushed me to the best I've ever been," he said with a smirk.
Godfather of Punk, indeed.

Bowie, Iggy and Reed all collaborated with each other in the early 70s, crafting a string of genre-defining albums that would go on to influence virtually *all* of the bands that made up the first wave of punk rock. Bowie had *Heroes* and *Low*, Iggy and The Stooges had *Raw Power* and later The Iggy Pop solo album *The Idiot* (both of which were produced by Bowie) and Lou Reed had *Transformer* and *Berlin.*

Glam/Proto-Punk Essential Tracks:

1. Now I Wanna Be Your Dog - Iggy & The Stooges
2. Rebel, Rebel - David Bowie
3. Vicious - Lou Reed
4. Personality Crisis - The New York Dolls
5. Sweet Jane - The Velvet Underground
6. The Next Big Thing - The Dictators
7. Get Down and Get With It - Slade
8. 20th Century Boy - T. Rex
9. In Every Dream Home a Heartache - Roxy Music
10. Suffragette City - David Bowie

Chapter 2: Building An Empire of Destruction

Let's Build a Home: CBGB and The Roxy

In the mid-70s, while literally thousands of people in cities all across the world were starting bands that were destined to be a part of a full-scale musical and cultural revolution, two cities quickly emerged as the twin focal points of punk rock: New York and London. You can pretty easily trace the development of both scenes by taking a look at the earliest bands and the two clubs that allowed them the freedom to be themselves.

New York in 1973 was a scary place to be. Riddled with crime and violence, it seemed like the only people left in the city were the absolute dregs of society. The bums, the weirdoes and the flat-out insane were all that remained after years of white flight to the suburbs. If you've seen Taxi Driver, you've got a pretty decent idea. So when Hilly Kristal opened up shop at 315 Bowery, his idea of a nightclub showcasing country, bluegrass and blues was flat out ridiculous. Nevertheless, the mighty CBGB went down in history anyway as the first club to give stage time to the strange new music brewing in the city.

The Ramones, the band at the epicenter of the CBGB scene, featured four young hoodlums in leather jackets loudly playing the simplest songs imaginable at an unbelievably frenetic pace. A typical early set for the group would last around 15 minutes, with a non-stop guitar assault broken up only by the occasional shout of "1,2,3,4!" by Dee Dee Ramone, the band's bass player.

Heavily influenced by the gutter-glam rock of The New York Dolls, the members of The Ramones decided to double the speed and lose the makeup. For anyone around to see their early shows, it was a revelation. Somewhere between the hard-edged streetwise strut of *53rd and 3rd* and the brazen call to action of *Blitzkrieg Bop*, something clicked. The rallying cry "Loud, Fast Rules!" would become a central tenet of all punk rock to follow, right up to the present day. The Ramones played at CBGB 74 times in the second half of 1974. Rock historians agree that The Ramones changed the course of popular music forever.

The Ramones were undoubtedly the most famous punk band to come out of the CBGB scene of the mid-70s, but they were only part of the picture. Pioneering groups like Television, Wayne County & The Electric Chairs and Suicide were all early performers at the club. New York City was not an easy place for an unsigned band to get a gig, and these bands were *weird.* Hilly Kristal probably didn't expect his club to give birth to the most explosive music ever produced, but by giving these bands an opportunity to compete for the spotlight, that's exactly what happened.

Suicide, a 2 piece act featuring Alan Vega on vocals and Martin Rev on synthesizer and drum machine specialized in droning, frightful soundscapes. Their 10 minute opus *Frankie Teardrop* is a truly terrifying song. They fit in perfectly with the transsexual Wayne County, who crafted an equally frightening stage show built around his incomplete gender reassignment. The Ramones seemed positively quaint by comparison.

The list of bands that played in the early days of CBGB reads like a who's who of American punk rock: Television, Patti Smith, Richard Hell, Talking Heads, Devo, Blondie and The Fleshtones all made multiple appearances at the club in its infancy. CBGB was also instrumental in the development of New York hardcore in the late 70s and early 80s. More on that later.

London in the 70s was arguably worse. An economic recession coupled with a garbage strike lent the normally well-kept city an air of hopelessness and anger. The glam rock scene had largely fizzled out, leaving a whole lot of bored, frustrated kids with little to do but collect welfare and start bands with a new, more aggressive sound and attitude appropriate to the garbage heap they'd inherited.

The jumping off point for punk rock in London was the first performance by The Ramones in the city. Held on July 4th, 1976, their gig at the Roundhouse was attended by the founders of dozens of seminal punk bands. Some of the leading London punk bands had already formed, but the amateurish, adrenaline-fueled Ramones proved that music was something they could do immediately, warts and all.

The legendary Roxy opened its doors in late 1976, immediately attracting hundreds of like-minded kids who were sick of the pretentious prog-rock popular in London at the time. Bands like Pink Floyd and Led Zeppelin were quickly discarded in favor of a new wave of groups with names like The Clash, The Damned, The Buzzcocks and The Slits.

During its early days, the club's DJ, Don Letts, wasn't able to play any punk records during the times when the bands weren't playing; they didn't exist yet. Letts, the son of Jamaican immigrants, filled the silence of The Roxy with the sounds of dub reggae instead, inspiring a punk rock love affair with Jamaican music that can still be heard today in the hybrid ska-punk scene.

A lot of these seminal shows would only exist as memories today were it not for the quick thinking DJ Don Letts, who trained a super-8 camera on the stage and the audience for most of 1977. His home movies, eventually released as *The Punk Rock Movie*, are a priceless document of the period, with early performances of classic songs like *Oh Bondage, Up Yours!* by X Ray Spex, *White Riot* by The Clash and *No Brains* by the somewhat lesser-known Eater.

While the club only remained open for a little over a year, virtually all of the marquee names in early British punk played there. The Stranglers, The Police, The Adverts, Wire and The Sex Pistols all shared the same tiny stage before the lights went out for good in early 1978.

CBGB and The Roxy Essential Tracks:

1. Blank Generation - Richard Hell & The Voidoids
2. Now I Wanna Sniff Some Glue - The Ramones
3. Psycho Killer - Talking Heads
4. Frankie Teardrop - Suicide
5. See No Evil - Television
6. I Live Off You - X Ray Spex
7. Neat, Neat, Neat - The Damned
8. White Riot - The Clash
9. Orgasm Addict - The Buzzcocks
10. New Town - The Slits

The Sex Pistols: The Filth, The Fury and The Fashion

Though they weren't the first punk band (and were certainly not the last), the mark on modern music that The Sex Pistols made can't be understated. They inspired countless bands with their antiauthoritarian lyrics and their explosive career trajectory. It's easy to argue that the initial sound of punk rock follows a pretty clear path straight from 50's rock n roll to 60's garage rock, followed by 70's glam and proto-punk. What's even easier to trace is the attitude and fashion: every bit of that comes from the mighty Sex Pistols.

Malcolm Mclaren, the onetime manager of The New York Dolls, left America and returned to London in 1975. He ran a clothing store with his girlfriend, fashion designer Vivienne Westwood. At first, they called the store Too Fast To Live, then renamed it Let It Rock. By the time a young man named Steve Jones started coming around and pestering Mclaren to manage his new band, the shop was called, simply, Sex.

At first, Mclaren wasn't remotely interested. The band wasn't exceptionally talented. Steve Jones was a mediocre guitar player and an even worse singer. The other members, drummer Paul Cook and bassist Glen Matlock, were better, but the music was middle-of-the-road pub rock. Mclaren wanted controversy; he wanted style. These guys had none of that.

One day, a teenager with green hair and an angry stare sauntered by the shop wearing a Pink Floyd tshirt with the words "I hate" scrawled above the logo. Mclaren remarkably quickly installed him as lead singer, christening him Johnny Rotten on account of his ridiculously bad, decaying teeth.

It was a lucky break for Mclaren and the others that Rotten was an excellent writer with a unique and decisive worldview, a pretty rare thing for a teenager. He quickly wrote lyrics to the group's instrumentals, resulting in a fiery blend of anger both personal and political. Almost as soon as the band began playing regular gigs, kids flocked to the shows to hear wild new songs like *Anarchy in the UK* and *Bodies*. Though painfully shy at first, Rotten quickly developed a confrontational stage presence that set a new standard for what a frontman could be.

Rotten's clothing style, ripped up t-shirts put back together with safety pins and suit jackets deconstructed in a similar way, became the style du jour among the band's followers. Seizing the opportunity, Mclaren and Westwood began copying his clothing and selling it to the fans in their store. Soon, it was easy to spot a punk rocker on the street; you only had to look for the safety pins and bondage pants.

While The Ramones, outside of New York City, remained relatively unheard of by the American masses, The Sex Pistols quickly became a household name in England. Tabloids and traditional newspapers reported on their every move. When they signed their first recording contract with EMI in

1976, they were labeled a curiosity. Shortly thereafter, they appeared on Britain's version of The Today Show, hosted by a man named Bill Grundy.

A last-minute replacement for fellow EMI band Queen, The Sex Pistols brought along a few friends for the interview, and after Grundy hit on Siouxsie Sioux (one of the women in their entourage and the future founder of Siouxsie and the Banshees), the resulting string of obscenities from the band headed into living rooms across London. The broadcast went down in history as "The Grundy Incident."

The next day, newspapers across England appeared with headlines like "The Filth and The Fury!" and "Fury at Filthy TV Chat." The tabloids turned against the group, causing most of their *Anarchy in the UK* tour dates to be cancelled. Effectively banned from playing live, EMI released them from their contract after the political pressure became too much for the company.

"They are unbelievably nauseating," said Greater London Councilman Bernard Brook-Partridge. "They are the antithesis of humankind. I would like to see somebody dig a very, very large, exceedingly deep hole and drop the whole bloody lot down it."

This was just the controversy Malcolm Mclaren was hoping for. He began fielding offers from other record companies and ousted the group's bass player, replacing him with Sid Vicious, a so-called Sex Pistols superfan. By this point, Malcolm didn't care that Sid didn't have the slightest clue how to play the bass. He had the right look: spiky hair, a leather jacket and a stage presence straight out of the Johnny Thunders/ New York Dolls playbook.

Around this time, dozens of punk bands seemed to sprout up out of nowhere. People were inspired by the group's uncanny ability to scare conservative society while rekindling the *danger* that rock n roll had lost. Bands like The Buzzcocks, X Ray Spex and Slaughter & The Dogs managed to secure major-label contracts almost within weeks of forming.

The Sex Pistols secured another crucial label deal with A&M in March of 1977 and prepared to release the groundbreaking single *God Save The Queen* in time for the Silver Jubilee, a countrywide celebration of the anniversary of Queen Elizabeth's coronation. 25,000 copies of the single were pressed before executives at A&M demanded they be removed from the label just six days later. Most of the singles were destroyed.

Thankfully, Virgin Records signed them for real shortly thereafter and sent *God Save The Queen* off to the record pressing plant. Of course, factory workers staged a mass protest over the record and initially refused to produce it, owing to the controversial content that was decisively antigovernment. They eventually relented, and the record quickly rose to the top of the charts.

The group released their only studio album, *Never*

Mind The Bollocks, in late 1977 before embarking on a disastrous tour of the US. Within three months of the record's release, the group had broken up, leaving a new crop of bands to fill the void. By early 1979, Sid Vicious was dead, and Johnny Rotten had formed Public Image, Ltd, a visionary post-punk group.

Sex Pistols and Friends Essential Tracks:

1. Anarchy in The UK - The Sex Pistols
2. Hong Kong Garden - Siouxsie and the Banshees
3. No Feelings - The Sex Pistols
4. Public Image - Public Image, Ltd
5. No Brains - Eater
6. God Save The Queen - The Sex Pistols
7. Ready, Steady Go - Generation X
8. Personality Crisis - The New York Dolls
9. Cranked Up Really High - Slaughter & The Dogs
10. London Girls - The Vibrators

Like Wildfire: Punk Rock Spreads Across The World

By 1977, the stage was set for a worldwide musical revolution. As if by magic, punk rock bands formed and flourished in almost every corner of the world. Inspired by The Sex Pistols and The Ramones, kids in the outer reaches of the cultural landscape dedicated themselves to the style and sound of punk rock. Just like in the 60's, they practiced in garages and played small shows for friends. Where substantial label interest couldn't be found, bands pressed their own records, sold their own t-shirts and, in a lot of cases, staged private shows at rented halls. The DIY ethic flourished.

In Los Angeles, the newly-christened Darby Crash hooked up with high school friend Pat Smear and formed The Germs. They recorded their first single, *Forming,* soon after, long before bothering to learn how to play or sing. Crash developed an Iggy Pop-inspired stage presence, cathartically cutting himself and smearing peanut butter all over his body in front of wildly enthusiastic audiences. The group quickly garnered a fierce reputation, forcing the police to take notice. The band and its fans were declared a gang by the LAPD, a fact they considered a badge of honor.

The Germs left an indelible mark on Los Angeles and the punk rock world at large. Their aggressive sound was a direct precursor to the hardcore sound, exemplified by several Los Angeles bands formed in their wake, notably fellow L.A. bands Black Flag, The Weirdos and The Circle Jerks.

In San Francisco, bands like The Nuns and The Dead

Kennedys gained worldwide attention for their sardonic blend of anti-establishment politics and humor. The Dead Kennedys were also a driving force in the early days of California punk, releasing wild, controversial songs like *Holiday in Cambodia* and *Kill The Poor* on their own independent label, Alternative Tentacles.

Like The Germs, The Dead Kennedys were also a constant target for police in San Francisco. In fact, their third album, *Frankenchrist*, was the subject of one of the last significant obscenity trials in the United States. A painting included as a poster inside the album was deemed pornographic and harmful to minors. Their offices were raided by the police numerous times in the weeks and months leading up to the trial. They eventually won the case, but Alternative Tentacles was almost bankrupted in the process.

Even further north, punk rock secured a foothold across Canada with groups like Teenage Head, The Diodes and The Viletones. One of the higher-profile Vancouver punk bands, The Skulls, formed after the members witnessed a Ramones show in the city.

While they toured pretty consistently for a couple of years, even recording a demo tape including the classic track *Fucked Up Baby*, it wasn't until they disbanded and formed two new bands, D.O.A. and The Subhumans, that Vancouver punk certainly took off. Songs like a re-recorded *Fucked Up Baby* and *Smash The State* were far more aggressive than The

Skulls had been. D.O.A.'s second album, *Hardcore '81,* is credited with giving the harder-edged sound its name.

Northern Ireland also got in on the action in 1977. Right in the middle of "The Troubles", two competing bands formed: Stiff Little Fingers and The Undertones. With songs like *Alternative Ulster* and *Suspect Device*, Stiff Little Fingers helped to publicize their nation's plight to the world at large. By contrast, The Undertones had a more personal approach. Songs like *Teenage Kicks* and *Jimmy Jimmy* heavily influenced the later pop-punk of bands like Blink-182 and Green Day.

Long before Crocodile Dundee, a Brisbane band named The Saints became Australia's leading cultural export. Formed in 1974, by 1976 the group unleashed the classic single *I'm Stranded*, becoming the first punk group outside the US to release an album, beating out more notorious bands like The Sex Pistols and The Clash by several months. Though it would take awhile to reach the rest of the world, their music has had a lasting influence. The Saints resisted the fashion side of punk rock, preferring a low-key style of dress and performance that presaged the street punk and Oi! movements.

However unlikely it seemed at the time, punk rock soon found its way to Japan. The Star Club, undisputed leaders of Japanese punk, formed in Nagoya in 1977. Their first album, 1978's *Hot and Cool*, had a distinctly British-influenced sound. Lead singer Hikage established himself as a cultural icon in his home country. He continues to perform to captivated audiences all over Japan.

The Star Club weren't the only purveyors of punk rock in the land of the rising sun, however. SS were early leaders of the Japanese hardcore scene; The Blue Hearts and Bomb Factory stuck with a more Ramones-esque style. Inspired by the no-wave bands from New York, groups like Friction and Kadotani Michio came up with a frenetic brand of noise-punk that continues to have a wide audience in Japan to this day.

Finland had Eppu Normaali and Briard, who released

the excellent *I Really Hate Ya* in 1977. Briard and another Finnish punk band, Pelle Miljoona Oy, would eventually combine forces to form the most famous Finnish band of all time: the glam-rock inspired Hanoi Rocks.

Most of these bands recorded their music in English, presumably in an attempt to garner the widest possible audience. One notable exception to this trend was France. Bands like Oberkampf and Metal Urbain crafted punk rock specifically for a french-speaking audience. Their debut single, 1977's *Panik,* somehow managed to find a home on dozens of punk rock compilations, cementing their reputation the world over. Stinky Toys' *Boozy Creed* also managed to find an international audience, though it was recorded in English, a rarity for the band.

Perhaps the most remarkable of the international second wave punk rock bands, Chainsaw formed in Belgium in 1977. They recorded just one 7 inch EP before disbanding. The *See Saw* EP contained only 4 tracks, but every single one of them is note-perfect. Released on a small, independent label, *See Saw* is now a highly sought-after collectible among punk rock record collectors.

International Punk Rock Essential Tracks:

1. Fucked Up Baby - D.O.A.
2. Hello New Punks - The Star Club
3. I Really Hate Ya - Briard
4. Boozy Creed - Stinky Toys
5. Panik - Metal Urbain
6. Z'Heroes Guts - Chainsaw
7. Hito ni Yasashiku - The Blue Hearts
8. Oh, Canaduh - The Subhumans
9. I'm Stranded - The Saints
10. Alternative Ulster - Stiff Little Fingers

The Only Band That Matters: The Clash Break The Mold

Though they only existed as a band for a little over 10 years, The Clash were (and remain) the undisputed kings of punk rock. Their early singles were met with immediate praise and wonder by both fans and the UK music press. Though it would take a little while, they also managed to attract a loyal (and sizeable) following in the US. With a perfect blend of progressive politics and raw power, The Clash have managed to influence just about every single band that formed in their wake.

In 1976, just as bands like The Buzzcocks and The Damned were beginning to find their way, a group of art school dropouts led by guitarist Mick Jones and bassist Paul Simonon began toying with the idea of forming a punk band. Like most of the other early punk groups, they'd been inspired by watching an early Sex Pistols gig. They quickly lured singer Joe Strummer away from his pub-rock band, the 101ers.

"Once we had Joe on board it all started to come together," said Simonon.

Quickly rising to the top of the early UK scene, the group released their first single in 1977. *White Riot,* a pretty typical-sounding early punk song, quickly rose to number 34 on the pop charts, but the band were just getting started. Eschewing the angry, nihilist lyrics typical of the first wave bands, the group made a point of stressing their own diverse cultural and musical tastes. Their debut album, released just a few months later, would include a heavy reggae influence, most notably on *Police and Thieves*, a cover version of a popular Junior Murvin song.

The album hit number 12 in the UK, though CBS Records initially declined to give it an American release. By the time CBS relented, the record had become the highest-selling import album in US history. *(White Man) In Hammersmith Palais*, released as a single in 1978, was another hit for the group, and their first foray into ska. By the time their second album, *Give Em Enough Rope*, was released, the group were chiefly immune to categorization, though they continued to align themselves with punk rock for the duration of their career.

By 1980, music journalists were routinely referring to the group as "the only band that matters." Lyrically, the group continued their support for progressive politics and human rights, notably on *London Calling*, the group's third album. Strummer's lyrics on *London Calling* ranged from heavy-handed discourses about racism and drug abuse to the proliferation of nuclear power. *Spanish Bombs* dealt with the ongoing fallout from the Spanish Civil War.

In keeping with their anti-establishment reputation, The Clash decided that *London Calling* should be priced as a single album even though it was a two-record set. When the group initially approached CBS Records with the idea of a two-for-one, the company refused. A compromise was reached, and the company allowed them to include a free 12-inch single with the album, so the band included 9 additional songs on the "single" and had the album pressed before the record company noticed the trick.

Ironically, the most well-known song on the album isn't even listed on the credits. *Train in Vain*, an uncharacteristically pop-leaning love song, was supposed to have been included as a free giveaway in an issue of the British music magazine NME. When plans were scrapped, the song was tacked onto the end of the second disc. *Train in Vain* peaked at number 23 on the Billboard Hot 100, the group's highest charting single in America at the time.

1980 saw the release of *Sandinista!,* widely considered their most ambitious work. Released as a triple album, the record included 36 tracks, many of which saw the group veer even further from the stereotypical punk rock sound of the time. The album included experiments with dub reggae, jazz, gospel, calypso and rap, a first for a rock band. Tracks like *The Magnificent Seven* and *The Call Up* would receive heavy airplay in dance clubs around the world, despite the fiery, anti-establishment tone of the lyrics.

As with *London Calling,* the group decided to sell the record at a reduced price, reportedly striking a deal with CBS to forego royalty payments on the first 200,000 copies as a safety measure. Luckily for them, the record sold 500,000 copies in the US alone.

By 1982, internal strife was beginning to rip the band apart. Their drummer, Terry Chimes, developed an intense addiction to heroin and was replaced just after the completion of their 5th album. *Combat Rock*, released later that year, would prove to be their most commercially successful record. Their first single-record album since 1978, *Combat Rock* was conceived as another double album, though plans were scrapped after Terry Chimes' exit.

Lead single *Should I Stay Or Should I Go,* was an immediate hit in the US, and the band's profile was raised significantly. A US tour saw the group routinely performing for sold-out crowds of 20,000 or more. The second single, *Rock The Casbah*, was an even bigger hit. Despite lyrics about the censoring of western music in modern-day Iran, the song's infectious groove helped propel it to the top of the charts. In keeping with their populist aesthetic, the record opens with one of their most fervent political statements. *Know Your Rights* remains one of the band's most potent tracks, with Joe Strummer's assertion that every human being has three "rights", which are:

1. The right not to be killed. (Murder is a crime, unless it is done by a policeman, or an aristocrat.)

2. The right to food money. (Providing of course, you don't mind a little investigation, humiliation, and, if you cross your fingers, rehabilitation.)

3. The right to free speech. (As long as you're not dumb enough to actually try it.)

Over the next year, the band fell apart, releasing just one more album. 1985's *Cut The Crap* is the only album in the group's catalog to be met with critical disdain. Recorded without founding guitarist Mick Jones, the remaining members reportedly only recorded it because they owed CBS Records another album. It promptly faded from view, and The Clash decided to bow out gracefully.

"There had been a lot of intense activity in five years," Strummer said. "Secondly, I felt we'd run out of idea gasoline. And thirdly, I wanted to shut up and let someone else have a go at it."

The Clash Essential Tracks:

1. Safe European Home
2. (White Man) in Hammersmith Palais
3. Lost in The Supermarket
4. Straight to Hell
5. Spanish Bombs
6. Clampdown
7. Train in Vain
8. Rock the Casbah
9. Rudie Can't Fail
10. This is Radio Clash

Chapter 3: Turning Sound Into a Dollar Sign

Selling Out And Cashing in: The Go Go's, Billy Idol and The Police

Almost as soon as punk rock emerged, fans and bands alike became obsessed with the idea of authenticity. For every unique new voice in the community, a dozen pretenders lined up behind them, ready to profit from the latest trend. Punk rockers became vigilant defenders of their various creeds, deeming bands poseurs for any number of perceived infractions or insults to the greater community. This tug-of-war between new converts, dabblers and old school enthusiasts would repeat itself ad nauseum from 1977 right up until today.

Although most of the original punk bands were signed to leading labels (including The Sex Pistols, The Ramones and The Clash), selling out to mainstream corporations quickly became a pretty hot deal. Sometimes it was something as straightforward as a band exploring a new sound that earned the disdain of the punk community, though obviously The Clash were immune to this offense. Being labeled a poseur or a sellout remains one of the worst things that can happen to any self-respecting punk rocker. Let's take a look at a few of the more notable offenders of the early days. Decide for yourself if they truly deserve the scorn.

The Go-Go's became America's sweethearts in the early 1980's. Led by the twin songwriting talents of Belinda Carlisle and Jane Wiedlin, they became stars on the strength of catchy bubblegum pop songs like *Our Lips Are Sealed* and *Vacation* before disbanding in the mid 80's. While most people didn't realize it at the time, their perky image was a fabrication: all the members had been intimately involved in the early days of punk rock. Carlisle was even a member of the riotous, legendary Los Angeles band The Germs.

We Got the Beat, the band's most well-known song, was originally a pretty standard punk rock song, released in 1980 on the independent label Stiff Records, home of The Damned and Elvis Costello. It was a pretty substantial hit in the UK punk scene, so British fans were shocked in 1982 when a cleaner, polished version of the song became a worldwide hit, complete with an MTV video. So much for independence. Their public personas shifted away from their punk roots, and they became poster-girls for a new generation of shiny, happy shopaholic teens. Punk rockers cringed at the crossover success.

Another 80's star with punk rock roots and a questionable career trajectory, Billy Idol hit the big time in 1982 with the singles *White Wedding* and *Dancing With Myself.* Few Americans realized it at the time, but Idol had been the lead singer of one of the founding UK punk bands, Generation X. They'd had a huge UK hit with *Ready Steady Go*. In fact, a more punkish version of *Dancing With Myself* had been the breakout single from Generation X's last album, *Kiss Me Deadly*.

When Generation X broke up, Idol signed to Chrysalis Records as a solo artist and moved to New York, where he worked tirelessly with professional songwriters to craft a more pop-oriented sound. The plan worked and, for a time, Idol was the male equivalent to Madonna in the United States. The backlash in his home country was pretty severe: his highest-charting UK album, *Rebel Yell,* only managed to (briefly) hit number 37.

Though The Go Go's and Billy Idol began their careers as legitimate punk rockers before moving on to mainstream accessibility, one of the most popular groups of the 80's, The Police, obviously used punk rock as a means to an end, cementing their reputation as the first confirmed poseurs in the punk rock pantheon.

A trio of classically-trained jazz musicians, Sting, Stewart Copeland and Andy Summers formed their initially prog-rock leaning band in 1977. After catching wind of the punk rock craze that was sweeping the UK, the group released their first single, *Fall Out,* on Illegal Records. Deviously, the group paired the single with a decidedly punk-rock looking sleeve in order to attract sales from the throngs of UK kids who would purchase any music in the punk section of local record shops. The single sold well, and they embarked on a tour with Wayne County & The Electric Chairs.

The band soon abandoned the nervous, punky style that put them on the map in favor of a highly refined pop/reggae hybrid. Their first album, *Outlandos d'Amour,* sold millions of copies, largely on the strength of *Roxanne*.

The album was originally supposed to be called

Police Brutality, but once record executives heard the album, they decided that a romantic, French-sounding title would be a more appropriate sales tactic for the untapped American market. In what some described as a calculated move, *Roxanne* was banned from airplay on the BBC, owing to its thinly-veiled lyrics about prostitution.

"We had a publicity campaign with posters about how the BBC banned *Roxanne*," said Sting, in an apparent admission of controversy-courting.

The music press, however, saw right through them. Reviews of their first album (and its followups) were almost universally scathing, due in large part to their reputation as calculating businessmen.

"Its mechanically minded emptiness masquerading as feeling makes you feel cheated, worn out by all the superfluous, calculated pretense," said Rolling Stone Magazine.

Despite the negative publicity, The Police would go on to become one of the highest-selling bands of all time before breaking up in 1986. A reunion tour undertaken in 2007 was widely assumed to be solely for the money. It became the third highest grossing tour of all time with revenues of around $340 million.

Punk Rock Sellouts Essential Tracks

1. Lexicon Devil - The Germs
2. We Got The Beat (Stiff Records Version) - The Go Go's
3. Our Lips Are Sealed - The Go Go's
4. Ready Steady Go - Generation X
5. Kiss Me Deadly - Generation X
6. White Wedding - Billy Idol
7. Fall Out - The Police
8. Fuck Off - Wayne County & the Electric Chairs
9. Roxanne - The Police
10. Every Little Thing She Does Is Magic - The Police

Chapter 4: New Wave

And I Ran: New Wave and Post-Punk

While punk rock continued to inspire countless bands to form, many of them soon grew tired of the limited palette that the aggressive guitar-driven sound afforded them. Changing up the sound while retaining the punk rock emphasis on total artistic expression, this new crop of not-quite-punk groups conquered the world under the less threatening banner of new wave.

It's difficult to pinpoint exactly when and how the tide turned. Bands saddled with the new wave moniker came from a dozen different directions, from the sneering pop of Elvis Costello to the anglicized ska of The Specials, there truly isn't a stylistic origin other than the feeling of freedom that punk rock represented.

Elvis Costello was one of the first new wave acts to break out in a big way. A pub rock singer-songwriter in the mid 70's, he was signed to Stiff Records in 1977 on the strength of a not-at-all punk sounding demo tape. His first single for the label, *Less Than Zero*, was about half the volume and speed of the typical punk single of the day, but the lyrics were as punk rock as anything coming out of The Roxy. His first full-length, *My Aim Is True* was an instant hit, and is still regarded as one of the best debut albums of all time.

Although he wasn't exactly punk, he had the respect of punk rock audiences, a rarity at the time. In fact, when The Sex Pistols cancelled a performance on

Saturday Night Live at the last minute, Costello was offered as a last-minute replacement. His label asked him to perform *Less Than Zero* on the show, but Costello decided moments into the live broadcast to instead play *Radio, Radio*, a scathing indictment of corporate-owned radio stations. He was subsequently banned from SNL until 1989.

The Knack had a massive hit with *My Sharona* in 1979. While the song owed some of its style to punk music, the radio-friendly production owed more to The Who and other British Invasion bands. Soon, groups like The Knack and The Cars were supplanted by a new crop of hyper-stylish, synthesizer-loving British bands, helped along by a new American television channel, MTV.

When MTV premiered in 1981, new wave bands made up a whopping percentage of the videos played, raising the profile of new wave music considerably. It was just a happy accident, as British new wave bands had already made quite a few videos to be shown on the BBC, and at the time, MTV played whatever they were given. It took a few years for record companies to see the power of a popular video, but once they figured it out, we were all treated to ridiculous videos like *Safety Dance* by Men Without Hats. It only got worse from there.

Forgettable bands with names like The Human League and A Flock Of Seagulls would quickly enter the national consciousness and then disappear just as quickly. Just like with glam rock in the 1970's, a lot of these new bands adopted a genderbending fashion, replete with makeup for boys and short hair and pants for girls. It's for this reason that most new wave music wasn't taken particularly seriously by the music press at the time. By contrast, post-punk shared many of the same attributes (minus the makeup, usually) but was immediately greeted with respect and admiration.

Though they formed in 1976, right in the middle of the first wave of punk rock, Joy Division became the first band recognized as post-punk. Started in the depressing industrial city of Manchester, the group were inspired by a Sex Pistols gig in their hometown to form a band. While they were massive fans of punk rock, the members of Joy Division opted for a more atmospheric, morose sound. Led by singer Ian Curtis, who sang in a deep, haunting voice, the group quickly developed a rabid fan base with songs like *She's Lost Control* and *Transmission.*

A local talk show host, Tony Wilson, was so impressed with Joy Division that he formed a record label just to be able to work with the band. Factory Records would go on to be the most famous cultural institution to come from Manchester, putting out records by bands like A Certain Ratio and Happy Mondays.

Joy Division's first album, *Unknown Pleasures,* was released in 1979. The group embarked on a UK tour with fellow Manchester band The Buzzcocks. Though their profile was raised considerably by a cover story in NME, things soon soured for the band, as Ian Curtis was diagnosed with epilepsy after suffering a seizure on stage.

Despite the setback, Joy Division continued to grow in popularity. After completing recording sessions for their second album, *Closer,* the band were invited to tour the US for the first time. Sadly, the night before they were to leave for America, Ian Curtis committed suicide. *Love Will Tear Us Apart* became the group's biggest hit, released just days afterwards. The rest of Joy Division would go on to find massive success with New Order.

While Joy Division were certainly the most famous of the post-punk bands, they were by no means the only ones. Public Image, Ltd, Johnny Rotten's post-Sex Pistols band, had a Jamaican dub-inspired post-punk sound. Bands like The Cure and Siouxsie & The Banshees formed the core of what would later be called goth-rock.

Though far less successful commercially, The US was also home to a number of remarkable post-punk bands. Mission of Burma, The Minutemen, Husker Du, The Replacements, even R.E.M. were considered post-punk, at least initially.

The Birthday Party, an Australian post-punk band, were also influential. Led by the charismatic Nick Cave, the band put out the incredibly strange single *Release The Bats* in 1981. No-wave bands like Sonic Youth and The Contortions cite The Birthday Party's barely-controlled cacophony of noise as a major influence.

New Wave/ Post-Punk Essential Tracks:

1. Just What I Needed - The Cars
2. Less Than Zero - Elvis Costello
3. I Ran (So Far Away) - A Flock Of Seagulls
4. My Sharona - The Knack
5. Video Killed The Radio Star - The Buggles
6. Love Will Tear Us Apart - Joy Division
7. Blue Monday - New Order
8. Boy's Don't Cry - The Cure
9. She's Lost Control - Joy Division
10. Release The Bats - The Birthday Party

Big A, Little A: Anarcho-Punk

With the ascension of new wave, punk rock headed back underground. Though less visible to mainstream audiences, bands continued devoting themselves to the music, eschewing popular tastes in favor of regional, homegrown scenes built around a handful of truly dedicated bands. With aggressive music and even more aggressive politics, anarcho-punk was the antithesis of the largely forgettable new wave music that ruled the airwaves in the early 1980's.

None of these new ultra-politicized bands were as dedicated to the cause as the members of Crass. A rigidly anticapitalist group of artists, musicians and all-around troublemakers, the members of Crass came together at Dial House, a commune/art space on the outskirts of London. Lead singer Steve Ignorant had been inspired by first wave punk bands The Sex Pistols and The Clash into melding his peaceful anarchist philosophy with this new music. After all, The Sex Pistols had released *Anarchy In The UK;* they must be kindred spirits.

Ignorant and the other members of Crass, disappointed by what turned out to be simple appropriation of anarchist symbols for shock value, decided to take matters into their own hands. They quickly recorded *The Feeding of the 5000,* putting it out on Small Wonder, a local independent label. After plant workers refused to press the album due to the perceived blasphemy on the opening track, *Asylum*, the album instead began with *The Sound of Free*

Speech, 2 full minutes of silence. Disappointed with the record label experience, they founded their own company, Crass Records. They expressed their disgust on *Punk Is Dead:*

"CBS promote the Clash, but it ain't for revolution; it's just for cash. Punk became a fashion just like hippy used to be, and it ain't got a thing to do with you or me."

The group's philosophy resonated with a pretty large subset of UK punk rockers, inspiring more than a few bands to embrace the anarcho-pacifist aesthetic. Bands like The Subhumans (not to be confused with the Canadian band of the same name) and Flux of Pink Indians became leading lights in the scene. The freewill philosophy that these bands espoused can be pretty neatly summed up by the lyrics of the Crass song *Big A, Little A:*

"Be exactly who you want to be. Do what you want to do. I am he and she is she, but you're the only you."

Crass Records ended up releasing albums by a wide sampling of anarcho-punk bands. Their first non-Crass release was *You Can Be You* by a teenage runaway named Honey Bane. She was staying at The Dial House while on the run from British juvenile authorities. The single was printed with the words "Pay no more than 65p" right on the sleeve, forcing record stores carrying it to keep the price low. 65p was, at the time, around half the usual price of a single. Crass Records would continue to do this for nearly every release, a tactic borrowed by Ian Mackaye for his bands Minor Threat and Fugazi and his own independent label Dischord Records.

One night, the members of anarchist collective Zounds were traveling through London when their van broke down. By sheer coincidence, they were helped out by members of Crass, who invited them back to Dial House. While repairing their van, the two bands bonded over shared anarchist ideals, and though they couldn't have been more different musically, Crass would record and release Zounds' excellent debut EP, *Can't Cheat Karma*. The EP, and especially the title track, are noted for being prime examples of the optimism that permeated the anarcho-punk scene initially. Within a few years, police harassment would turn many of the bands angry and militant.

Crass (and Crass Records) adopted a highly specific visual style that stood in stark contrast to the mohawk and safety pin fashion of the day. All members adopted black clothing in a military-surplus style, thereby keeping themselves anonymous and ensuring that no one member would be seen as the leader. Record sleeves and promotional material developed a highly specific, stenciled look. World-renowned graffiti artist Banksy cites Crass and their associated imagery as a primary influence.

Another of the most impactful anarcho-punk bands, The Subhumans, also formed their own record label. Bluurg Records released seminal Subhumans albums like *Worlds Apart* and *Rats*, but also albums by The Gits and Conflict. The Subhumans (alongside Crass) would help to form a national network of fans, supporters and distributors, proving that the DIY ethic could sustain an entire subculture.

The anarcho-punks championed causes ranging from animal rights to election reform. Sustainable living was a primary concern, as was the elimination of racism. The anarcho-punk movement had the distinct disadvantage of being railed against by both extremes: right-wing fascists hated their ideas about total freedom; left-wingers felt that they went too far with their proselytizing.

Though the subgenre has faded in and out of favor since 1977, dozens of bands take a heavy influence from anarcho-punk bands. One of the most critically-acclaimed modern punk groups, Florida's Against Me! consider themselves anarcho-punk, though they were briefly signed to a major label. The "direct action" ideas espoused by the original anarcho-punk bands can still be seen today in the activism of groups like the Animal Liberation Front and other so-called ecoterrorism groups.

Anarcho-Punk Essential Tracks:

1. Can't Cheat Karma - Zounds
2. Get To Work On Time - The Subhumans
3. Big A, Little A - Crass
4. You Can Be You - Honey Bane
5. Some Of Us Scream, Some Of Us Shout - Flux Of Pink Indians
6. Only Human - Rudimentary Peni
7. Sheep Farming In The Falklands - Crass
8. No - The Subhumans
9. You Cannot Win - Conflict
10. Persons Unknown - Poison Girls

Out Of Step With The World: Hardcore And Oi!

By the 80's, punk rock had been co-opted by large corporations and sold back to fans as new wave. The Sex Pistols had long since self-destructed and The Ramones were doing their best to get themselves a top ten hit, even recording with famed pop producer Phil Spector in an attempt to give their sound a radio-friendly sheen. Punk rock didn't seem to mean much anymore. Then, along came hardcore punk to scare everyone all again.

Largely a suburban phenomenon, hardcore took its anti-establishment cues from the first and second waves of punk, but the music was a lot more aggressive. Where safety pins and wild colored hair were the order of the day, hardcore kids adopted a low-key style of close cropped hair, t-shirts and (often) military boots. Shows were routinely shut down by the police, and bands were classified as gangs.

Welcome to the 80's.

Heavily localized scenes formed, built around a handful of bands from each city. Los Angeles, San Francisco, New York, Boston and (especially) Washington, D.C. all had thriving hardcore scenes by the early 1980's. Eschewing key labels, the DIY directive of anarcho-punk continued, with most of the bands self-releasing singles and albums and undertaking tours of the US in vans, crashing on fans' floors for the duration. A few enterprising people formed their own labels. Ian Mackaye (of Minor Threat and Fugazi) started Dischord Records; Greg Ginn (of Black Flag and Gone) started SST.

Black Flag were perhaps the most notorious of the hardcore bands. Often referred to as the godfathers of hardcore, Black Flag initially formed in Hermosa Beach, California. Guitarist Greg Ginn and original singer Keith Morris developed a brand of frenetic, driving rock that combined the dirge of heavy metal with dynamics and chord changes that were sometimes compared to jazz. They practiced for several hours each day to perfect the sound, writing anti-establishment lyrics critical of modern America.

Keith Morris left the band to form The Circle Jerks in 1979. He was eventually replaced by Washington, D.C. fan Henry Rollins. This lineup released the classic album *Damaged* in 1981, then embarked on a seemingly endless tour. The aggressive music garnered them aggressive fans, and the group were routinely attacked on stage and off at venues across

America.

Growing tired of the violence in the hardcore punk scene, the members of Black Flag soon grew their short hair out and began slowing the tempo of their songs, adopting a sound that came closer and closer to the heavy metal that hardcore fans hated. This sound can be most easily heard on songs like *My War* and *Nothing Left Inside.*

Black Flag were among the most visible, but they were only one of dozens of hardcore bands to come out of the Los Angeles scene. Circle Jerks, Bad Religion, T.S.O.L. and The Adolescents would also leave an indelible mark on the city.

Washington, D.C. also had an influential hardcore scene. Led by the all-black Bad Brains, a slew of bands took off there in the early 80's. The Bad Brains' single *Pay to Cum* is considered one of the best hardcore singles of all time. Minor Threat, another D.C. band led by Dischord Records head Ian Mackaye, were instrumental in the formation of the straight edge scene, with their singles *Out Of Step* and *Straight Edge* espousing a fervent anti-drugs and alcohol worldview.

Minor Threat would have a substantial influence on the Boston Hardcore scene, with bands like SS Decontrol and Negative FX forming the "Boston Crew", an extraordinarily violent arm of the straight edge movement. Boston Crew members would routinely hand out beatings to punk rockers they saw using drugs or alcohol, leading Boston to acquire a reputation for punk-related violence that the city has yet to shake off.

Across the pond, British bands were also developing a harder edged style. Upset that the UK punk movement had become too academic and had lost all relevance for working class kids, bands began working hard to differentiate themselves from what they saw as pretentious art-for-art's sake.

Adopting Doc Marten boots and Fred Perry shirts like the (non racist) skinheads who had earlier dominated Britain's working-class subculture, bands like The Cockney Rejects and Angelic Upstarts forged a sound that stripped all accoutrements from punk rock. Chainsaw guitars and shouted vocals were the order of the day, coupled with lyrics about police oppression, soccer and sex (in no order.)

Pretty quickly, football hooligans, racists and other assorted miscreants attempted to usurp the original working-class intent of Oi! attending shows and causing all manner of trouble. While most of the bands maintained left-wing politics, the far right managed to infiltrate and disrupt the movement. A highly influential Oi! compilation, *Strength Through Oi!* even had Nicky Crane, a local neo-nazi leader, on the cover, causing the mainstream press to assume that Oi! was a right-wing movement.

Things came to a head on July 4th, 1981, when a UK concert featuring The Business, The 4-Skins and The

Last Resort was interrupted by local Asian kids, who had assumed (wrongly) that the concert was a neo-Nazi recruiting effort. They had reportedly found some white power graffiti nearby. The resulting riot lasted for five hours, injuring over 100 people. The concert hall burned to the ground.

Around this time, some working-class punks became disgusted with the right-wing reputation that Oi! had garnered. A new crop of bands, led by groups like The Exploited and GBH, began calling themselves street punk. Stylistically similar to Oi! street punk bands retained the working-class focus while distancing themselves from right-wing politics. They also adopted a more sinister punk look: mohawks and leather belts became the norm. *Punk's Not Dead*, the title of an early Exploited single, became a rallying cry for the ages.

Hardcore, Oi! and Street Punk Essential Tracks:

1. Rise Above - Black Flag
2. Deny Everything - Circle Jerks
3. Punk's Not Dead - The Exploited
4. Straight Edge - Minor Threat
5. Pay To Cum - Bad Brains
6. Working - Cock Sparrer
7. England 5, Germany 1 - The Business
8. Fighting In The Street - Cockney Rejects
9. Feel Like A Man - Negative FX
10. TV Party - Black Flag

Chapter 5: The Rebirth of Punk

Self Esteem: The Punk Rock Revival

While punk rock had certainly had its ups and downs in the 70's and early 80's, its power to change the world eventually seemed to wane. Edged out by hip-hop and boy bands, punk seemed to disappear by 1988. In reality, it was there all the time, lying in wait. And in 1991, it began climbing back out of the underground with a vengeance.

Two hugely different bands came to epitomize the heights to which punk rock could rise in the nineties. One of them was Fugazi, a group of Washington, D.C. purists led by former Minor Threat singer Ian Mackaye. The other, a trio of kids from the outskirts of Seattle who grew up on a combination of hardcore and metal: Nirvana.

Soon to be crowned leaders of a nonmovement the newspapers dubbed "grunge", Nirvana was a fairly typical northwestern punk/hard rock band who had signed to a major label at the urging of New York post-punk pioneers Sonic Youth. Their second album, *Nevermind,* would go on to sell over 30 million copies, surprising pretty much everyone on the planet. They were at the right place at the right time.

Major record labels began signing a new crop of bands, many of whom (Bad Religion, Green Day, Weezer) would never have been given a chance beforehand. They reinvigorated punk rock for an entirely new generation of kids. Though some may argue that Nirvana were not a punk band in the strictest sense of the word, one listen to songs like *Drain You* or *Lounge Act* will immediately prove that

Nirvana's style owed as much to Black Flag as it did to Black Sabbath.

"Punk is musical freedom," said singer Kurt Cobain. "It's saying, doing, and playing what you want."

Fugazi, by contrast, wouldn't have been caught dead on a major label. Lead singer Ian Mackaye had made sure of that by forming Dischord Records in the early 80's, while still a member of seminal hardcore band Minor Threat. Teaming up with former Rites Of Spring singer Guy Picciotto, Fugazi would release the seminal ode to DIY *Waiting Room* in 1988 before recording their debut full-length, *Repeater*. Though not an instant hit, *Repeater* began climbing the Billboard chart shortly after Nirvana hit critical. It would go on to sell over 2 million copies, a record for an independent label at the time.

Fugazi were a band full of idealists. Constantly touring, they made sure that prices for their concert tickets were kept low, typically 6 dollars or less. They also dedicated themselves to exclusively playing all-ages shows, making sure young kids could hear them. Like Crass Records before them, the band also went out of their way to make sure their records were affordable, adding the words "This album is available for 8 dollars postpaid from Dischord Records" to the covers of each of their albums.

Pretty quickly, other punk bands garnered national attention. The pop-punk scene had been gaining underground momentum since the mid-80's with bands like The Descendents and Screeching Weasel. They would spawn a whole new generation of bands like NOFX and The Offspring, who would in turn spawn unlikely hitmakers like Rancid and Green Day.

Both Rancid and Green Day came out of what was known as the Gilman Street scene, formed around an all-ages punk club in Berkeley, California. Rancid began their life as Operation Ivy, a ska-punk band that only existed for two years, breaking up before the release of their debut album, *Energy*. The record would go on to sell over half a million copies on the independent label Lookout! Records.

Gilman Street would help to turn the tide away from the drugs and violence that had sullied punk's reputation in the early 80's. The all-ages club enforced a strict set of rules for the bands that played and the fans that came to see them. No drugs, no alcohol, no violence and no racism were tolerated. Bands were not allowed to be associated with a major label, and, before allowing a band to play, they had to submit lyrics to the owners to make certain that they were not homophobic, racist or misogynist. It sounds almost fascist today, but these rules helped maintain a haven for the kids who made punk rock their lives.

Green Day, inspired by seeing performances by Operation Ivy at Gilman Street, formed in 1987. At first, they were unremarkable. Like most other Gilman Street bands, they released EP's and singles on Lookout! Records and toured the country in a van, playing shows for small crowds along the coasts.

Their second album for Lookout! *Kerplunk* was a moderate independent success, selling around 50,000 copies. Reprise Records took notice and in the wake of the breakout success of Nirvana, signed them.

"I couldn't go back to the punk scene, whether we were the biggest success in the world or the biggest failure," said lead singer Billie Joe Armstrong. "The only thing I could do was get on my bike and go forward."

Green Day's leading label debut, *Dookie*, was released in 1994. An instant success, the album spawned the unlikely hit singles *Longview, Basket case* and *When I Come Around.* While early fans accused the band of selling out, Green Day never looked back, and have continued to be one of the highest-profile bands on the planet.

A few months after *Dookie* was released, The Offspring broke out with *Smash*, released on the independent label Epitaph. On the strength of singles *Come Out And Play* and *Self Esteem,* the album sold upwards of 12 million copies, still a record for an independent album.

The dam burst and soon bands like NOFX, Bad Religion, Pennywise and Rancid were household names. The commercial fortunes of punk rock peaked in the late 90's with Blink-182; a pop punk band formed by two friends in 1992. Their debut album, *Cheshire Cat,* came out in 1994, but it was the follow-up, 1997's *Dude Ranch* that put the band on the map. By the end of the 90's, they were the biggest selling band on the planet.

The alternative was now the mainstream.

Punk Revival Essential Tracks:

1. Basket Case - Green Day
2. Lamar Vannoy – The Bouncing Souls
3. Waiting Room - Fugazi
4. I Wanna Riot - Rancid
5. Drain You - Nirvana
6. Dammit - Blink-182
7. Do What You Want - Bad Religion
8. Leave It Alone - NOFX
9. Self Esteem - The Offspring
10. Merchandise - Fugazi

A Message to You, Rudy: 2 Tone and Ska-Punk

As unlikely as it sounds quite a few bands found mainstream success by melding punk rock music with Jamaican ska. Bands like The Mighty Mighty Bosstones and Reel Big Fish managed to briefly crack the pop charts in America before fading back into obscurity.

While the music was initially confined to a culturally isolated Jamaica, ska was popularized in Britain by West Indian immigrants right around the time that punk rock exploded onto the scene. Don Letts, DJ at the infamous Roxy, is usually credited with exposing the nascent punk rockers to Jamaican music by playing dub reggae and ska over the club's PA in between bands. Some punk fans took a shine to it. 2 Tone was born.

Led by bands like The Specials and Madness, 2 Tone ska was a wholly integrated musical phenomenon. Most bands included both black and white musicians and attracted an audience of mods, rude boys and skinheads, British subcultures with no real American counterparts. The Specials' 1979 hit, *A Message to You, Rudy*, was an early success. Madness made a splash in America with the ubiquitous *Our House*.

While mainstream success in Britain and The US was fleeting, other countries took the ball and ran with it. Blechreiz and The Busters swept Germany in the early 80's with songs like *Out Tonight* and *Ruder Than Rude*. Skarface were a popular ska-punk band in early 90's France. Australia had The Allniters, who had a number one single with *Montego Bay* in 1983.

The underground nature of the ska scene paralleled the DIY movement in punk rock. Small, independent labels like Moon Ska and Unicorn Records flourished when cardinal labels ignored the phenomenon. Ska undoubtedly shared the spirit, if not the aggressive sound of punk rock. Soon, the two sounds would merge, causing a brief explosion of popularity in America.

The Mighty Mighty Bosstones began life as a traditional Boston hardcore band, Gang Green. Lead singer Dicky Barrett, long a fan of 2 Tone music, decided to blend hardcore with a ska influence, resulting in frenetic, danceable songs like *Someday I Suppose* and a wild cover of the Minor Threat classic *Think Again.* Signed to Mercury Records in the mid-90's, the group were featured in the movie *Clueless.* A few years later, they hit the top of the charts with *The Impression That I Get.* Lesser known bands like The Pietasters and The Scofflaws toured the country, spreading the gospel of ska-punk across the country.

The success of bands like The Mighty Mighty Bosstones was a direct result of the out-of-nowhere rise of No Doubt, a southern California ska-punk band led by singer Gwen Stefani. Their 1995 album, *Tragic Kingdom,* was a landmark for the genre. Supported by the singles *Spiderwebs, Just a Girl* and *Don't Speak*, the album would go on to sell 10 million copies, touching off a brief American fascination with ska-punk before retreating into the underground scene.

2 Tone and Ska-Punk Essential Tracks:

1. A Message to You, Rudy - The Specials
2. Montego Bay - The Allniters
3. Think Again - The Mighty Mighty Bosstones
4. Stuff - MU330
5. Spiderwebs - No Doubt
6. Mirror in the Bathroom - The English Beat
7. Sound System - Operation Ivy
8. Three Minute Hero - The Selecter
9. Sell Out - Reel Big Fish
10. Something Better - The Pietasters

Chapter 6: Punk...Present and Future

I Was A Teenage Anarchist: Emo, Screamo and Punk Rock Today

With the rise of file sharing in the early 2000's, punk rock's audience grew by leaps and bounds. Independent labels, long frustrated by weaker distribution than their corporate competition, no longer had to fight for record store space. Everything moved online. Suddenly, punk rock bands didn't even need a label at all, just a Myspace or Facebook page. The Internet became the principal equalizer. Every punk band from here on out would rise or fall based on the strength of the music, not record industry machinations.

Right as this shift was happening, a new buzzword started creeping up into the national consciousness: emo. Short for emocore, the bands that became the vanguard of modern punk rock mostly came up from this more emotional subset of hardcore music. Inspired by early post-hardcore bands like Sunny Day Real Estate and Jawbreaker, who melded aggressive punk with a yearning and intelligence rarely seen in the genre, bands like The Promise Ring, Alkaline Trio and Jimmy Eat World formed and quickly became underground favorites in the late nineties.

Stylistically varied, the rise of emo can nevertheless be traced back to two albums released on paramount labels that flopped at the time, but ended up influencing everything that came after. The first, Weezer's *Pinkerton*, had been expected to be a blockbuster. Weezer had hit the big time with their debut album and its breakout single, the instantly catchy *Buddy Holly*.

Instead of releasing another album full of catchy surf-pop, the band instead created one of the most raw, personal records ever released. Songs like *Tired of Sex* and *El Scorcho* were the antithesis of their formerly radio-friendly sound. The record was so badly received at first that lead singer Rivers Cuomo put the band on hiatus and returned to college.

"It's like getting really drunk at a party and spilling your guts in front of everyone and feeling incredibly great and cathartic about it, and then waking up the next morning and realizing what a complete fool you made of yourself," said Cuomo.

Bands like Taking Back Sunday and Dashboard Confessional disagreed, citing the album as a major influence. The idea of baring one's soul instead of crafting a song took hold. Jimmy Eat World, one of the more celebrated early emo bands, would release 1999's *Clarity*, their main label debut, in response.

Clarity also sold poorly and was largely ignored by the music press. The band were dropped from Capitol Records shortly after its release. Again, other bands disagreed with the poor reception and were inspired to take their music further.

Jimmy Eat World decided to self-finance their next album, *Bleed American*. Its lead single, the instant classic *The Middle,* was an unexpected sensation in the summer of 2002.

A more aggressive offshoot of emo, screamo started gaining momentum in the early 2000's. A dynamic, melodic style of punk, usually punctuated by periods of guttural screaming, bands like The Used and Hawthorne Heights are excellent examples of the genre.

Emo and its related styles are certainly the most visible new strains of punk, but they are by no means the only thing happening today. More traditional punk bands like Rise Against and A Day To Remember are far more popular than their 70's and 80's counterparts, but Florida punk band Against Me! are the new kings of the genre.

Formed in 1997 as a solo project for lead singer Tom Gabel, Against Me! quickly garnered a rabid following in the college town of Gainesville, Florida. Songs like *Baby, I'm an Anarchist* and *Sink, Florida, Sink!* melded the spirit of anarcho-punk with a distinct folk influence. Alongside other like-minded bands like Hot Water Music, they toured relentlessly, cementing a dedicated network of fans worldwide by 2005.

Like many punk bands before them, they eventually signed with a major label, though their first album for Sire, 2007's *New Wave*, was arguably even more angry and intense than their albums for indie labels had been. Still, the backlash came. Gabel and company responded with *I Was a Teenage Anarchist*, a scathing indictment of the narrow-minded punks who had rejected the band.

"It was a mob mentality, they set their rifle sights on me. Narrow visions of autonomy, you want me to surrender my identity. I was a teenage anarchist; the revolution was a lie," Gabel sang.

With his band riding the upper echelon of popular music, Against Me! singer Tom Gabel stunned the world in 2012 by announcing (In Rolling Stone) his intention to become a woman by undergoing sexual reassignment surgery. Rechristening herself Laura Jane Grace, the band continued to perform to vast audiences around the world. While Gabel's decision met with a few raised eyebrows in conservative communities, the punk rock world rose to defend and applaud the decision.

"Tom is displaying extraordinary courage by coming out as transgender after already establishing herself as a rock star," read a statement released by GLAAD. "For many of the band's fans, this may be the first time they're actually thinking about transgender people and the bravery it sometimes takes in order to be true to yourself."

It's that exact bravery that keeps punk rock, in all its forms, alive and breathing. Wherever there are kids who don't fit in, wherever they can find the courage to climb onto stages and make a joyful racket, punk rock music will inspire generation after generation to find their place in the world without being spoon-fed their culture. The punk rock of tomorrow might not look or sound like it has in the past, but it will undoubtedly remain a force to be reckoned with.

Emo, Screamo and Punk Rock Today Essential Tracks:

1. Bleeder - Alkaline Trio
2. Sweetness - Jimmy Eat World
3. Boxcar - Jawbreaker
4. Pints Of Guinness Make You Strong - Against Me!
5. The Taste Of Ink - The Used
6. You're So Last Summer - Taking Back Sunday
7. A Flight and a Crash - Hot Water Music
8. I Was a Teenage Anarchist - Against Me!
9. Architects - Rise Against
10. Understanding in a Car Crash - Thursday

Cover image © hurricane - Fotolia.com

Printed in Great Britain
by Amazon.co.uk, Ltd.,
Marston Gate.